CW01573011

HUMAN DEVELOPMENT

NICHOLAS TUCKER

CHiLDHOOD

Human Development
CHiLDHOOD

Adolescence

Adulthood

Childhood

Old Age

Throughout this book, a child is referred to as female. This is purely for ease of style and, unless otherwise stated, all information applies to both males and females.

Series editor: Marcella Streets
Series design: Helen White
Series consultant: Dr John Coleman

First published in 1990 by
Wayland (Publishers) Ltd
61 Western Road, Hove
East Sussex, BN3 1JD, England

British Library Cataloguing in Publication Data
Tucker, Nicholas
  Childhood. – (Human development).
  1. Childhood
  I. Title II. Series
  305.23

ISBN 1–85210–914–9

Phototypeset by Nicola Taylor, Wayland
Printed in Italy by Rotolito Lombardo
Bound in France by A.G.M.

CONTENTS

iNTRODUCtiON

The study of human development helps us to discover how a baby becomes an adult.

HOW DOES a helpless, new-born infant become a talking, thinking individual? How is it that two children with the same parents can be so different? The answers to these questions can be found through studying human development.

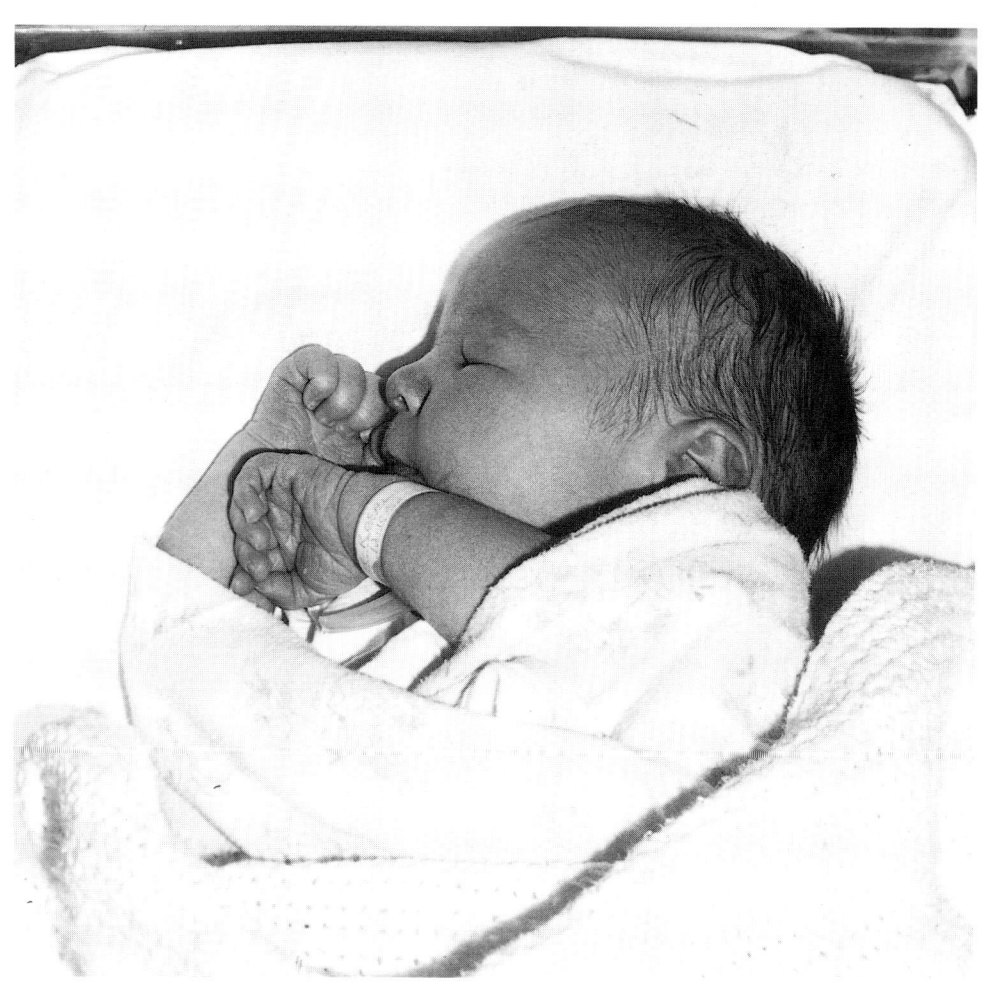

We all have some kind of idea of the stages a human being goes through in developing from a baby to an adult, and we usually recognize when something happens at an unusually early or late stage. For example, people are amazed to learn that Mozart had already composed his first concerto by the time he was seven years old. We can recognize that this was an unusual achievement for such a young child. But why is it that he was so gifted musically? Did he inherit his talent from his parents, or could anybody be as good if they practised hard?

When we study human development, we try to discover the answers to questions like these. We also try to identify the general sequence of changes

Mozart was unusually gifted: he composed his first concerto at seven years old.

that human beings go through during their lives. As well as physical developments, such as learning to walk, we need to understand how children learn to solve problems, how their emotions develop and how they become sociable individuals.

Although most people experience the same basic process of human development – for example, we all learn to walk after we can sit upright – each of us is unique. People have different ideas and values; how do these differences come about?

To understand the ways in which human beings develop, we must first look at what influences our development. There are two major areas of influence: genetics and environment. No one is entirely sure how much each aspect of development is genetically determined and how much is due to environmental influences.

Genetics

While all human beings belong to the same species and therefore share certain characteristics (for example, we stand erect), each individual has their own combination of genes, which they inherit from their parents. Genes determine certain physical characteristics and may also play a role in other areas of development.

Genes are passed on in the following way. When a male sperm fertilizes a female ovum, the result is a single microscopic cell known as a zygote. This tiny speck contains the entire genetic code that helps determine what sort of person the cell will become. The code is carried by forty-six thread-like structures known as chromosomes – twenty-three coming from the mother and twenty-three from the father. These chromosomes are made up of DNA (Deoxyribonucleic acid), a chemical substance which, under a powerful microscope, looks like a spiral staircase. Each chromosome consists of small segments called genes; around 50,000 genes are located at various points on the chromosomes. If you think of the chromosome as a ladder, then genes make up its thousands of rungs.

Four days after conception the zygote has already divided into twelve to sixteen cells, using the original pattern of genes as a model for further growth. Some genes, known as dominant genes, are

A human being is at first a tiny cell, containing chromosomes. Each chromosome contains a part of the genetic code that determines what sort of person the cell will become.

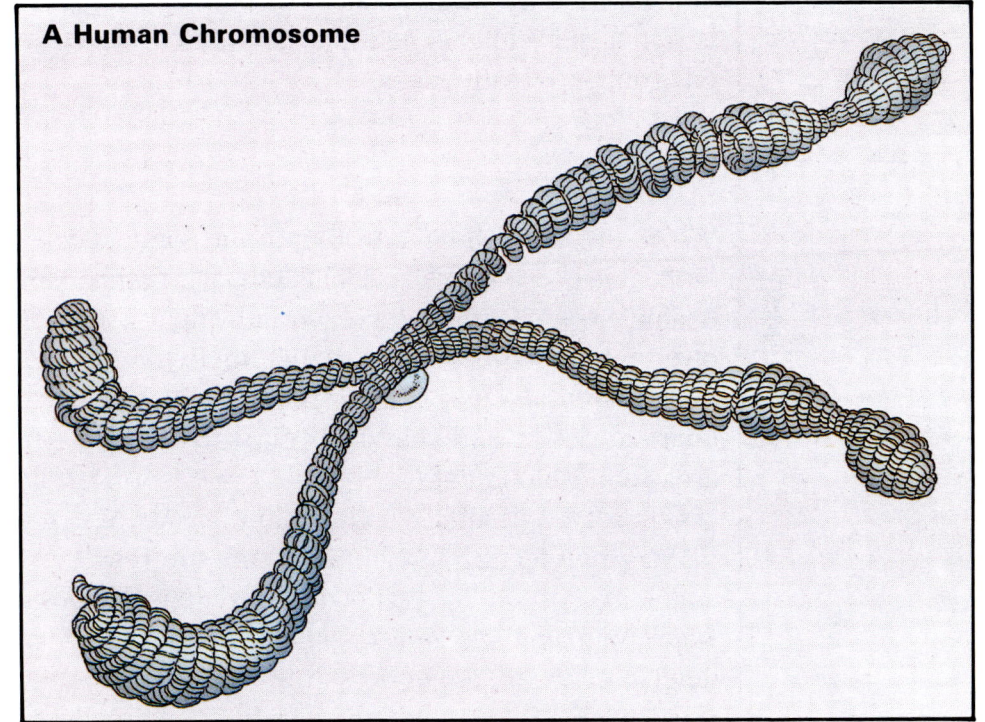

A Human Chromosome

Like most children, this child has inherited a unique combination of genes from his parents. (Only identical twins share the same genetic code.)

more powerful than others. They usually triumph over the weaker, recessive genes when they come into conflict. Brown hair, for example, is associated with a dominant gene, and fair hair with a recessive gene. This means that if one parent has brown hair and the other has fair hair, their children are more likely to have brown hair. Brown eyes and black skin are also controlled by dominant genes. In each case, the particular combination of the father's and mother's genes will create an individual who, while resembling their parents in certain ways, will be quite unique.

Genetically influenced characteristics are also passed down from grandparents to grandchildren, even though the parents themselves may not have inherited them. So while two dark-haired parents are likely to have dark-haired children, they may produce fair-haired offspring.

ENVIRONMENT

Some physical aspects of human development, such as height, are partly determined by genetic inheritance, but are also influenced by the environment, or surroundings, in which a person is raised. For example, a potentially tall child (in other words, someone with tall parents) may have her growth stunted by poor diet.

Environmental influences include family, culture, wealth, diet and health. The way a child is brought up by her parents can have a major effect on her. For example, a child whose parents are warm and loving may grow up to be more confident than a child with harsh, critical parents.

Each society has its own values and customs which are taught to children from an early age and which may continue to influence them for the rest of their lives. For example, in some cultures men and women are expected to do different types of work; this may affect the way in which children are brought up within that culture, and the expectations of those children in later years.

Within most cultures there is a social class system. Those at the top have a higher status, and often more wealth, than those at the bottom. The values, attitudes and expectations of people in one class may be very different from those in another.

All these aspects of the environment can affect the way in which human beings develop.

CONCEPTION TO BIRTH

It takes 38 weeks for a tiny human cell to grow into a baby that is ready for birth.

IN THE thirty-eight weeks from conception to birth, two tiny human cells combine and grow to produce a new and unique human being.

Foetal development

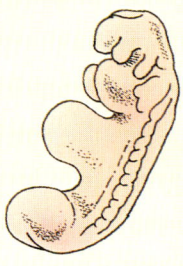

Weeks 4-5
By the fifth week the baby's nervous system is developing.

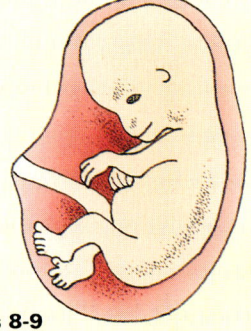

Weeks 8-9
At eight weeks the face, hands, feet and major organs have started to develop.

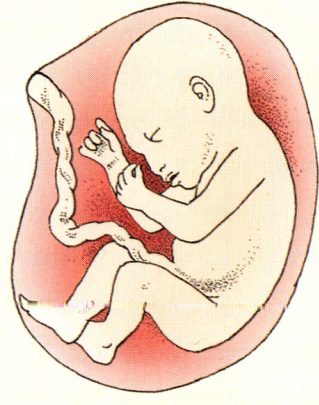

Weeks 15-22
By about the twentieth week the mother can feel her baby moving.

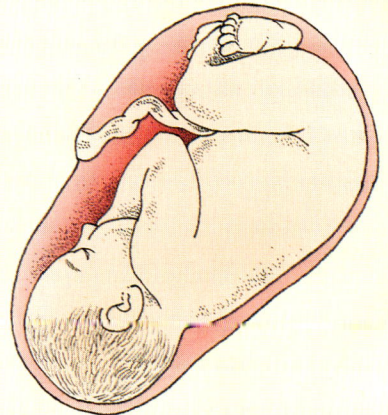

Weeks 31-40
During the last few weeks the baby gets plumper and is usually lying head downward, ready for birth.

A baby is created from two cells: a male sperm and a female ovum. Sperm are tiny and tadpole-like, with an oval head and thin tail. Genes are carried in the head of the sperm and thus passed on from father to child. A woman's genes are stored in the ovum, which is a minute egg-like structure.

iN THe uTeRUS

When an ovum is fertilized by a sperm following sexual intercourse, a single cell is formed, called a zygote. One week after conception the zygote will consist of around 150 cells. The number of cells continues to increase until a tiny human embryo is formed. The cells also produce the placenta, which helps the embryo to feed, breathe and get rid of waste matter through its mother while in the uterus. The embryo is linked to the placenta by an umbilical cord (which also grows from the zygote), and is protected by a bag of water, called amniotic fluid.

By the fifth week in the uterus the embryo's nervous system, heart and umbilical cord are developing. At six to seven weeks, small swellings (called limb buds) have appeared where the arms and legs will grow. After eight weeks the embryo is termed a foetus. By this stage, all the major organs – the heart, brain, lungs, kidney, liver and gut – are all developing. The face is slowly forming, with a mouth and tongue, and the beginnings of hands and feet have appeared. By the twelfth week, the foetus is fully formed, even though it is only around 56 mm long from head to bottom (about the size of a mouse). At twenty weeks the mother is able to feel the foetus moving inside her uterus and the heartbeat can be heard through a stethoscope.

During the remaining weeks the foetus grows and develops. At around twenty-six weeks, its eyelids open for the first time. If a baby is born before twenty-eight weeks' pregnancy, it does not stand a good chance of survival because its vital organs are not sufficiently developed, although specialized hospital care can help such babies survive.

MATERNAL HEALTH

A foetus draws its nourishment from its mother via the umbilical cord and placenta, so it is important to the foetus's health that its mother eats a well-balanced diet. Harmful substances, such as alcohol and chemicals from tobacco smoke, can pass from mother to foetus via the cord. Alcohol can stunt a foetus's growth and hinder brain development. Mothers who smoke heavily tend to have smaller-than-average babies because smoking reduces the supply of oxygen to the foetus. Oxygen is needed for the development of the foetus's brain cells, particularly during the closing stages of pregnancy. Heavy smokers also run a higher risk than non-smokers of having a stillborn baby.

It is also important for a pregnant woman not to suffer too much stress. Extreme fear, for example, can lead to restricted blood-flow to the uterus, which could deprive the foetus of vital oxygen.

Childbirth can be less worrying if parents have attended classes beforehand, where the woman is taught how to relax and her partner is shown

Opposite
Smoking during pregnancy reduces the supply of oxygen to the baby and can stunt its growth or damage its brain.

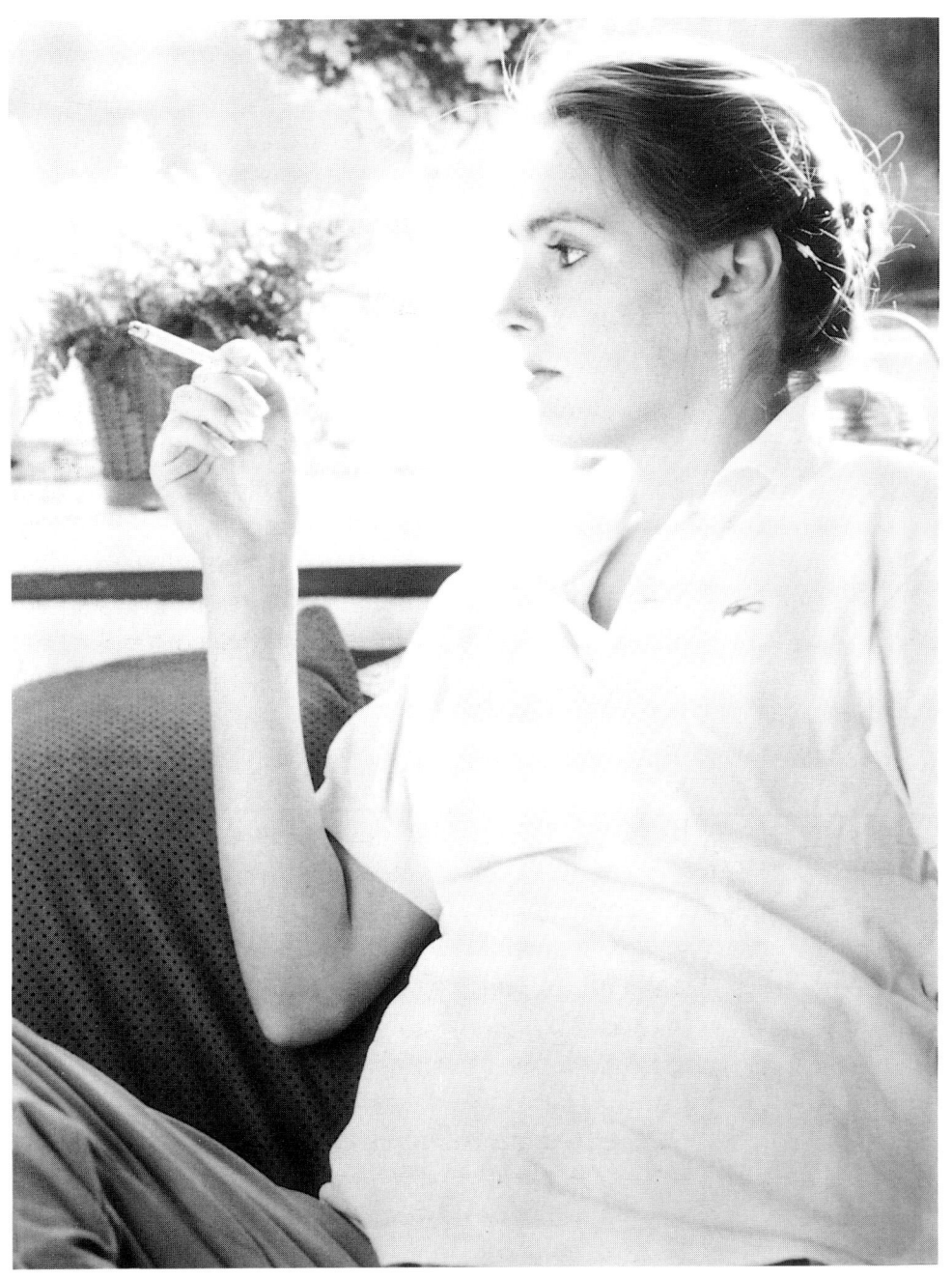

Special classes teach pregnant women how to relax during childbirth, and teach their partners how they can help.

how to help her during the birth. These classes are important, since a difficult birth can sometimes be dangerous for a baby as well as very distressing for the mother. A stress-free birth, on the other hand, makes an excellent beginning for the long years of parenthood ahead.

BIRTH

A normal foetus spends between thirty-seven and forty weeks in the uterus before birth. The process of giving birth is called labour. The muscles in the woman's uterus open the neck of the uterus and push the baby through the birth canal. This usually takes between four and twelve hours, although it can be much shorter or longer.

The beginning of labour is marked by either a small discharge of blood and mucus (called a show), or the breaking of the bag of water in which the baby has developed, or by regular and strong contractions (muscular spasms) of the uterus. The contractions start slowly but then become stronger, regular and more frequent. They open up the neck of the uterus wide enough for the baby's head to pass through. The contractions then push the baby through the birth canal (usually head-first) into the world. Too quick a passage can lead to serious pressure on the baby's head as it pushes through this narrow gap. But too slow a delivery can leave a baby deprived of oxygen.

In some cases a baby is not born in the normal head-first position but emerges instead with its buttocks first; this is known as a 'breech' birth. This can be dangerous if the baby experiences breathing difficulties. If this seems likely to happen, the baby may be delivered by Caesarean section instead. It is then taken out of the uterus through an incision in the abdomen.

This baby is being delivered by Caesarean section, which involves taking the baby out of the uterus via an incision in the mother's abdomen. This does not hurt because she is given anaesthetic.

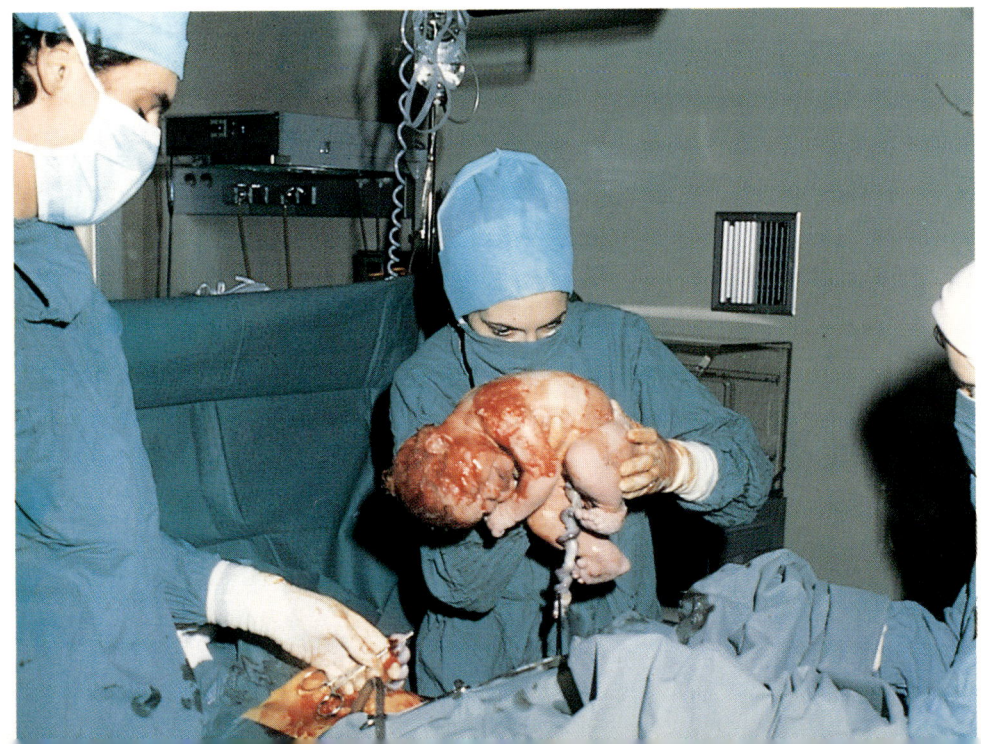

THE FIRST YEAR

THE FIRST year of life is a period of rapid development. At birth a baby is totally dependent on her parents, but by one year old she can usually move about independently and communicate some of her needs to others.

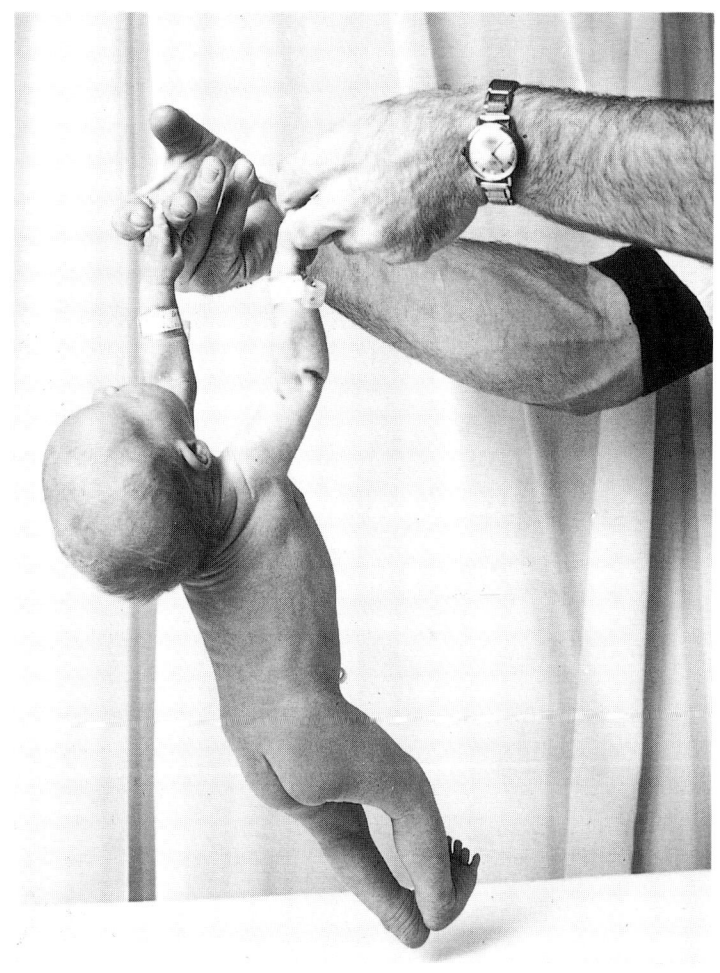

If you hold a new-born baby upright with her feet brushing a flat surface, she automatically makes walking movements. This is a reflex action.

Senses and Reflexes

A new-born baby can see, hear, smell, taste and feel. In addition she is born with a number of basic reflexes (automatic movements made without thinking). These consist of:

- **Falling reflex** Sudden movements that affect a baby's neck make her feel as if she might be dropped. This causes the baby to fling back her arms and bring them back together, as if catching hold of something.
- **Grasp reflex** If you place something – such as a finger – in a baby's hand, she grasps it automatically.
- **Rooting reflex** When touched on the cheek, a baby automatically turns her head in search of a nipple for feeding.
- **Startle reflex** When startled, for example by a sudden noise, a baby bends her elbows and clenches her hands.
- **Swallow and suck reflex** Babies automatically suck and swallow anything that is put into their mouths.
- **Walking reflex** If you hold a baby upright with her feet just brushing a flat surface, she automatically makes walking movements.

Some of these reflexes are more useful to the baby than others. If a baby were born unable to suck, she could not feed. On the other hand, no one is quite certain why the walking reflex is present at birth, for it disappears after about three months.

SLEEPING AND FEEDING

New-born babies often spend most of their time asleep – anything up to twenty hours a day – with feeding periods in between. They need a great deal of sleep so that they can build up the energy required to sustain their rapid growth.

For the first few days after birth the baby loses weight, but by the second week all this weight has been regained, and by the time the baby is five months old she has doubled her birth weight. During the first days after birth, the baby may have to be fed once every three or four hours, so great is her appetite.

Food will consist entirely of milk, either from the mother's breast or mixed from powder and fed from a bottle. Most doctors prefer mothers to breast-feed, since mothers' milk contains substances that give their babies immunity to certain diseases, but bottle-feeding can be just as good.

Breast-fed babies usually stay on an all-milk diet for up to six months, but bottle-fed ones are often fed puréed or specially-bought baby foods as well after around three to four months. This may consist of nothing more than one or two small teaspoonfuls each day, much of which is spat out at first.

PHYSICAL DEVELOPMENT

At first a new-born baby's body movements are very jerky. She has almost no control over her head, except when lying on her back, when she can move it just slightly. But by one month old, a baby can

Opposite
Babies are weaned from a bottle or breast milk on to solid food by being given a couple of teaspoonfuls of puréed food each day to begin with. This amount is gradually increased until the baby is having regular meals and wants her bottle or breast milk less frequently.

18

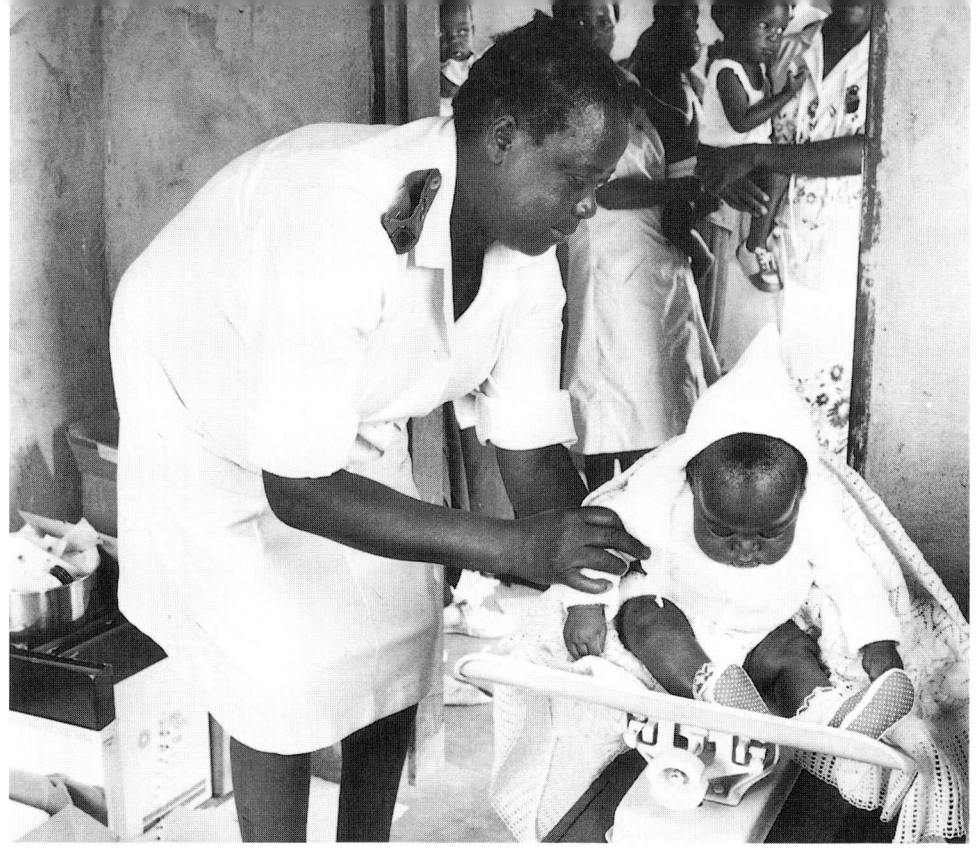

By the time a baby is five months old, she has doubled her birth weight.

generally lift her chin when lying in a prone position, and at two months she can lift her chest. At three months she can hold her head steady and also start reaching out for objects, although she usually misses them.

Physical development is rapid over the next four months. The baby learns how to roll from her stomach to her back, how to move objects from one hand to another, how to sit unsupported and eventually how to stand when held by an adult. Given a toy, she will now often look at it closely, sometimes putting it in her mouth. By eight months old, the baby may start crawling, or shuffling along on her bottom. She will also probably have her first teeth. Incisors (teeth used for cutting food) are the first to appear.

At around nine months old, a baby starts showing the first signs of genuine independence. She may try feeding herself with her own spoon. This is a messy business to start with but does encourage a baby's confidence in her own capabilities. Eventually a baby will learn to pull herself up, holding on to furniture, and may even take her first steps by the time she is one year old.

THE FIRST RELATIONSHIP

At birth babies cannot see more than 20 to 25 cm ahead. This is also the average length they are from their parent's face in the normal feeding position for breast or bottle. After six weeks or so a baby will look straight into her parent's eyes during feeding, and will watch their movements. If the parent moves her head when playing with the baby, the baby will often try to move hers in return. If the parent sticks out her tongue in a game, the baby may try to do the same thing. New-born babies can hear, and when a parent speaks or sings, the baby will often pause while this is happening, as if waiting her own turn in a conversation.

In these ways a baby builds up her first relationships with other human beings. Together she and her parents get to know each other. The baby learns how the parents look, act and feel; this will be her first introduction to human behaviour in others. The parents learn to assess the baby's moods, needs and progress. For example, they will eventually be able to establish when the baby is tired or ready for another game, or whether a

Parents have to get to know their baby's different moods. | certain way of crying means the baby is in pain or just hungry.

Baby and parent also have to work out a feeding rhythm that suits them both. If the baby swallows the milk too quickly, she will suffer from wind. If she drinks too slowly, she may fall asleep in the middle of feeds and so never really get enough. By getting to know what suits them both, parent and baby are laying the foundation for a sharing relationship that may persist for the rest of their lives.

social development

Social development involves learning the skills that enable people to live together with other members of their community. Although human beings are naturally sociable, they have to learn some social skills, for example how to share their possessions, what rules exist and what sort of behaviour is unacceptable to others.

By six weeks old, a baby is clearly interacting socially; she begins to show pleasure by smiling when people look at her. At three months, she may be ready for games of peek-a-boo, where an adult covers their face with their hands, then suddenly opens them, shouting 'boo'. As well as finding this very funny, a baby eventually learns from the game that, even when something has disappeared from view, it has not gone altogether.

Play is an important part of social development. Although children play for pleasure, it also helps them learn. Babies start to play at around three months old. At this age they like to handle objects, particularly those that are brightly coloured or make a noise. At around ten months they like putting things in containers, such as bags, and taking them out again. Skills such as stacking bricks help the baby develop physical skills she will require later in life.

eMOTiONaL DeVeLOPMeNT

Emotional development is affected by temperament and environment. Temperament is probably genetically inherited to some extent; some children are worriers, others are not; some babies are noisy, others are quiet. The hurdles and obstacles a child has to face while growing up have an effect on emotional development, however, as does the attitude of parents. Children need to build stron g bonds of affection with other people, particularly those who look after them. In infancy, these bonds are strengthened by touching, eye contact and familiarity. Without love and interest, a child will be insecure and unhappy; she may grow up unable to show affection herself.

LeaRNiNG TO THiNK

Before they have learned to talk, babies often get frustrated and angry at their inability to communicate their desires. This often results in temper tantrums. Babies learn to talk by listening to others and copying their sounds. To begin with, a baby responds silently to human speech, often smiling back or waving her arms when spoken to in an affectionate way. At three months she will start babbling back.

The noise babies make at this age is not easy to interpret, but if parents talk back to their child the baby is encouraged to go on trying, and eventually she will be able to make one or two sounds that seem like proper words. Sounds like 'dad-dad' and 'mum-mum' are made at around nine months old, and by a year children are beginning to understand that words have specific meanings and are able to follow simple verbal instructions. To begin with, a baby might use one word to cover a whole group of similar things: for example, 'cat' might be used for any animal.

every baby is different

An ordinary, healthy baby has been busily using the opportunities provided for her during her first year to start developing all the skills she is going to need in the future. In building up a secure relationship with their parents, babies create a safe haven from where they can learn to make sense of what they

Play is an important part of social development. By placing these balls on a stick, these children are practising co-ordination skills that they will need later in life.

see and hear around them. They also discover how to make noises closely resembling speech and begin to co-ordinate their movements through learning how to manipulate various objects during play sessions.

However, it is important to remember that each child develops at its own pace. Even from the earliest days some babies are beginning to show signs of what type of person they are going to be. Some may already be very active, moving their arms and legs around as best they can. Others prefer to lie still. Some may seem extra-fretful and easily upset, while others are altogether more at ease with life.

As they develop, some babies tend to mature faster than average. Others develop a little slower, or else show contradictory patterns: fast in some areas, slow in others. Some parents can become particularly competitive with each other about the speed of their baby's development. However it is a mistake to expect one baby to be at exactly the same stage as another simply because they are the same age, or to think that speed of development is a sign of superior intelligence. In the end, almost all babies grow up able to walk and talk like everyone else. But if parents are worried about their baby's rate of development, they can consult a doctor.

separation

Occasionally babies have to be separated from their parents at an early age. This may be for short or long periods. Parents who cannot look after their babies may decide to offer them for adoption or fostering. In many families a parent or baby may have to spend some time in hospital, or both parents may go out to work, leaving the baby in the care of someone else for part of the day.

The effect of separation on a baby varies from case to case and also depends on the amount of time spent apart. Generally, if the baby is left with someone who takes the time and trouble to care for her properly, she should not be harmed and will do just as well as if she were with her own parents. However, if a baby is left for hours without any stimulation and never made to feel part of a strong relationship, development may be impaired. Such a child may be slow to play, talk, walk or even laugh, because no one has ever shown any real interest in encouraging her to do so.

Of course, slow development due to lack of encouragement can also happen in children who are living with their parents.

*ea*RLY CHi*L*DH*OO*D: 1-5

DURING THE second year, a baby may grow only about 15 cm but she will change during this time from being a fat baby to becoming a leaner and more muscular infant.

Between one and five years old, children learn much through play.

PHY*Si*CaL D*e*V*e*L*O*PM*e*NT

One of the major developments during the second year of life is learning to walk alone (this happens at around thirteen months of age). At first toddlers are

28

unsteady on their feet and often hold their arms up to keep their balance. They find it difficult to stop or turn, and fall over frequently. By around eighteen months, a toddler can walk upstairs holding on to a rail and putting both feet on each stair. By two years old, she can come down in the same fashion and kick a ball without falling over. At two-and-a-half, she can jump and walk on tiptoe and six months later she can stand on one leg. By four she may be able to hop, and by five she may have mastered the skill of skipping.

Hand co-ordination skills also develop between the ages of one and five. At fifteen months a toddler can use a cup and spoon but often spills things. By eighteen months, she can feed herself properly and can also build a tower of three blocks. At the age of two, a toddler can turn handles, draw, and pull on her own shoes. By five years old, a child can usually dress and undress without help and eat with a knife and fork.

At around a year old, children cut their first molar teeth, followed by their canine teeth at eighteen months. By two-and-a-half years old, children usually have all twenty primary teeth. The permanent set of twenty-eight teeth will not appear until they are around six years old.

TOILET TRAINING

Most children do not start developing bowel and bladder control until they are around eighteen months old; many are not fully toilet trained until three years old.

Hand co-ordination skills develop considerably during early childhood. This boy has mastered the art of feeding himself.

Bowel control is usually achieved before bladder control. Once a child becomes aware of passing urine or stools, she begins to tell her parents when she has done so. The next stage is telling someone during the actual process. Eventually she will be able to tell someone in time to be taken to the lavatory or put on a pot.

Punishing or scolding a child for wetting or soiling herself before she has developed the muscles to prevent this is pointless. Even when they are toilet trained, children need to go to the toilet very quickly and do not always have time to tell someone. Scolding them for this merely destroys their confidence.

THE GROWTH OF LANGUAGE

By the end of the first year, babies may already be using simple single words. Very soon two words will be put together, as in 'All gone,' or 'What's dat?' After these phrases there will be first sentences, with the young child sometimes using new words she has made up. For example, she may say, 'The ball has goed,' instead of, 'The ball has gone'. What is impressive here is that, by trying to use the past tense, the young child is already showing that she has some inbuilt idea of grammar. Far from simply mimicking language heard around her in the way that parrots do, the child is actually building up her

Most children do not start to develop bowel and bladder control until they are around eighteen months old, and many are not fully toilet trained until three years of age.

language. This can lead to mistakes with words that do not follow ordinary rules of grammar. For example, a child attempting to put the word 'mouse' into the plural may say 'mouses' instead of 'mice'. Mistakes like this indicate how knowledgeable about the rules of language a child has already become, since in fact most English words do simply add an extra 's' in the plural. It is hardly the child's fault if she is more logical in her approach than the English language is.

This awareness of grammar is achieved without any of the lessons necessary when adults learn a new language. Instead, young children pick up the rules of language by themselves. If they happen to live in a home where two different languages are spoken, they will usually learn both of these at the same time.

While parents and older children do not have to teach a young child to talk because she learns through imitation, they can play an important part in encouraging her. Speaking slowly and with extra emphasis when chatting with the young will help them understand and learn.

Some parents believe that young children can learn to speak by watching television or listening to the radio. However, speech on television and radio usually goes too fast for a young child's understanding. When talking or reading to a young child, it is important to pace this to suit the child and to pause to answer questions. Questioning is an important part of development; the number of questions asked increases with age, particularly those beginning with, 'Why?'

By four years old, a child has usually mastered the basic rules of grammar and her speech is fairly easy to understand. However, children mispronounce many words because they have difficulty in making certain sounds and so substitute easier ones.

EMOTIONAL DEVELOPMENT

No matter how friendly and good-humoured they may be, all young children tend to be naturally selfish. If they see something they want, they will often simply take it. If another child tries the same thing with one of their toys, they may get very angry. Young children usually only see things from their point of view. This is known as egocentrism. Developing a true understanding of the needs and feelings of others involves mental skills they will not achieve until later. Before young children finally understand they cannot always get their own way, many of them have tantrums. These can be embarrassing for parents when they take place in

Young children tend to be naturally selfish and take what they want without thinking of others.

Young children may need a lot of reassurance to overcome their fears.

front of other people, but even so they should not be given in to.

Children are often fearful about certain things that seem harmless to older people. At night they may insist on a light inside, or just outside, their room. They may wake crying from a bad dream, demanding to be let into their parents' bed for comfort. It is important for parents to be understanding about this, though never to the extent of always giving in. Dreams can be very terrifying to young children, as they often cannot sort out what is real and what they have dreamt.

Other terrors may also develop, such as children fearing they might slip down the plug hole along with the bath water. This is because they are not yet capable of the logical thought necessary to understand that, in reality, this would be impossible. Also, the noise the water makes as it goes down can be frightening.

Children may need a lot of reassurance to overcome their fears. Without such support a nervous child may have problems later on, with additional fears emerging.

JEALOUSY

Jealousy is a natural human emotion. It is often displayed by children when a new baby is born into the family. They may feel that this baby will be competing with them for their parents' attention and so feel insecure, hitting, biting, demanding attention and moping. This behaviour usually disappears in time. Parents can help by reassuring the child that she is loved and wanted, even when she behaves badly.

LEARNING TO TALK

With the growth of language comes the growth of thought. To begin with, young children make instant judgements about their world, generally on the basis of one particular detail they pick out at first glance. For example, young children may believe that big coins are always worth more than smaller ones, because they have learned elsewhere that big is often thought superior to small. If their older brother or sister is taller than they are, they may then believe that tall people are always older than shorter ones, even when comparing a tall father with a shrunken grandfather.

In such cases, children are generalizing from one situation to what they see as a similar one. This is quite natural; learning to take into account more than one leading feature of an object or person when making judgements or comparisons is a complex skill that develops later.

Often, children attribute human characteristics to non-human objects. Their reasoning seems to be as follows: because I have parents, eyes, a nose and a mouth, then so too do trains, cars, aeroplanes and anything else that can move around. A child may think that because she has learned to talk to others, animals can too.

Once more, it would be pointless to insist that they are mistaken. Until their thinking skills develop further, they should be given credit for making imaginative efforts to understand the world around them, even if they are often wrong.

sex Differences

At around the age of three or four years, children become aware of the physical differences between males and females, and by the time they are five years old they can clearly distinguish between males and females.

Some people claim that girls are better than boys at language and that boys have superior

mathematical skills. However, if this is so, it may well be because that is what is expected of them and because they are encouraged in these different areas from an early age. The same argument applies to aggression. Some people believe that boys are naturally more aggressive than girls, while others argue that boys are merely imitating the way they see men behaving on television, in films and in comics, or behaving in a way that is expected of them. For example, when boys fight adults often say, 'Boys will be boys'.

Playing in a group teaches children important social skills, such as how to get on with others.

PLaY

Much of the time between one and five years old is spent on different forms of play. This is a vitally important way in which children learn about themselves, others and their surroundings. No one has to teach a child to play; it is something that comes naturally. But it can and should be helped by the

By treating soft toys like babies, children are practising being parents.

provision of play materials, as well as by general encouragement.

Some play will be to do with learning various important physical skills. Playing with sand and water, for example, will teach a child how to make different shapes out of mud, pour from one container to another, and how to carry quite heavy loads without it mattering too much if things spill and make a mess. Wooden bricks teach skills of grasping and letting go, both essential in order to develop the light touch needed to perform more delicate actions. Throwing and catching a ball teaches co-ordination between hand and eye movements. Learning to thread a needle or complete a simple jigsaw puzzle teaches the fine physical skills necessary for precision work later in life.

Other types of play teach different skills. Pretend play, often involving dressing up, provides children with the chance to imitate various adult skills, ranging from household jobs to more elaborate actions, sometimes inspired by what they have heard in stories or seen on television. In this way, children can experiment with many different types of adult behaviour.

When games involve other children too, important points about how to get on socially may also be absorbed. When they first get involved in group games, children are usually very demanding, always wanting the best parts for themselves and apt to be impatient when waiting their turn. But once it becomes clear that other children will not tolerate this sort of behaviour, children have to curb their normal 'I-want-it-now' attitude.

Soft toys and dolls offer comfort to children, particularly when they are feeling tired or insecure. Such toys also provide opportunities for infants to start practising their own parent skills, using toys as substitute babies. For more active moods, trolleys and bicycles can be ideal. On quieter occasions, safety scissors, paints, paste and paper enable young children to start making their own simple playthings or paintings – another important step forward in building their confidence, and increasing manual dexterity. Easy board games offer valuable experience in learning how to follow simple rules, take turns, and cope with the painful business of occasionally losing to others.

CHiLDHOOD: 5-7

BETWEEN THE ages of five and seven, most children start school. Some will already have attended nurseries or playgroups, but even so the first days of school can be frightening for young children. From the security of home, they are suddenly launched into new, noisy and sometimes confusing surroundings.

These young children are practising hand co-ordination skills.

Instead of having an adult more or less to themselves, children will have to share their teacher with many other children. The teacher may not be as attentive and appreciative as those adults the child has been used to at home. In addition the young child may be taunted by other pupils, or find she sometimes has no one to play with.

In response to these changes, children in their first few weeks at school sometimes long to be back with their parents, from whom they may never have been separated for more than a few hours before. Some children may never really enjoy school, but the majority welcome the chance of making friends while also discovering exciting new opportunities for play. Climbing apparatus, sand-pit play and swimming all help develop social skills. In this way, many infants come to enjoy their new independence. At home they may also try to become more grown-up in matters such as learning how to undo buttons or tie up their own shoelaces.

FIRST LESSONS

Some people wonder whether infants ever do much more during their first years than play. But play is nature's way of preparing young people for later life. The beginnings of reading, writing and maths can all be found in games played at school during this time. So early lessons at school are best introduced through play, in order to make them both interesting and meaningful to the young. For example, learning how to balance different sized rods on either side of a scale, with each rod standing for a particular number, can act as an excellent playful introduction to maths. At this age children find it easier to think about things they can actually see, rather than things they have first to imagine, or work out from what someone else has told them.

Children's verbal skills need encouragement at school during these years. This is not just a matter of them listening to what the teacher is saying, then acting accordingly. They need to be encouraged to speak up for themselves, and to answer questions. Verbal skills gained at this age will make it much easier for them to take an active part in lessons later. Those who remain silent often get overlooked in a busy classroom, and sometimes pass the time by day-dreaming rather than by concentrating on their lessons.

FIRST FRIENDSHIPS

A child's first friendships are often made with children who live nearby or sit next to them in school. Young children are often used to hearing only their parents' views, and a friend can offer a child a new perspective. Up to that moment, parents or older brothers and sisters will have seemed the ultimate source of wisdom to a young child. But now the class teacher and friends may also be quoted as notable authorities.

By around seven years old, children start copying each other in dress and habits. Normally peaceful children may suddenly develop a new tough side to their personalities in imitation of other children their age. Children like to feel the same as others. Feeling or looking different may become a major worry that will often persist into adolescence and even into adulthood.

Forming successful first friendships is an important part of any child's growth and

independence from the family. Some quarrelling and bad feeling between children is inevitable as they adapt to this stage of their development, but on the whole most children enjoy each other's company at this age.

By the time they are seven years old, most children can read a little.

LeaRNiNG TO ReaD

Learning to read is an important stage of development in childhood. Children can be encouraged to take an interest in books by being read to from an early age. Listening to stories teaches concentration skills. Looking at picture books encourages young children to try to interpret what is happening and to ask questions.

By seven years old, most children can read a little, although those who have been slow in talking tend to be slow readers. Slowness in learning to read affects other areas of children's learning; they may find it difficult to follow written instructions and directions for other work at school.

iNTeLLecTuaL DeveLOPMeNT

Some research has shown that children who do well in school tend to come from parents who take an active interest in their offspring. This is because conversation and general verbal stimulation at home during infancy are the best preparation for success in education. Learning to ask and answer questions, talk to a sympathetic audience and hold their own in an argument all help to prepare infants for the later demands of the classroom.

Between the ages of five and seven, children's memory increases, as does their ability to concentrate. A child's speaking vocabulary may now be between 8,000 and 14,000 words, with some children learning anything up to twenty-two new words each day. They can also now put together much longer sentences by inserting relational phrases such as 'more than', and linking phrases with words like 'because' and 'if'. In this way they can express far more complex ideas than before. Their new vocabulary also makes it much easier for them to discuss things that either happened in the past or else are expected to take place in the future.

Children of this age also begin to show more sensitivity to the needs of others in conversation.

When talking to much younger children, seven-year-olds may now use shorter sentences and a slower mode of speech, just as adults do. When needing help, they now find it easier to transfer these needs into effective requests for aid. Some of the lisping and bouts of stammering heard before will also begin to disappear. They should also know how to write their own names and how to solve a few easy sums.

Despite all these impressive developments, children of or below seven years old still find much about the world very confusing. Adult reasoning will often remain hard to follow, and most things that happen during the day will simply be taken for granted. Living very much in the here and now, young children sometimes find it difficult to think ahead to the coming afternoon, let alone the next day or week.

As they become more aware of the feelings of others, children can become quite protective of younger brothers and sisters.

Asking questions helps to extend children's vocabulary, as well as their general knowledge. Between the ages of five and seven, a child may learn up to twenty-two new words a day.

A child's knowledge of the world is very limited at this stage of development. Geographically they still believe their own town or village to be the absolute centre of things, with other counties or countries only dimly thought about, if at all. As for history, they may very well be able to imagine a time long ago when their grandparents were once young. But any time beyond that tends to swim together into one general period of history where dinosaurs, Jesus Christ and Napoleon all lived together. Such misunderstandings are common at this age. The next great leap forward in intellectual development will see many of these infantile ideas gradually replaced by more grown-up notions, as children begin to think more like adults in a number of important ways.

LATE CHILDHOOD: 7-11

UNTIL THEY are seven, children tend to think the world is either just as it seems at first glance or else as they would like it to be.

If young children want the sun to shine for their birthday, they may think that if they wish hard enough this will happen. If one event happens straight after another – for example a child sneezes and it then immediately starts raining – they may imagine that the first event actually caused the second.

However, at the age of seven years old children's thinking gradually starts to become more logical. For

Developments in memory and logical thought enable children to master quite complicated board games.

Practical experiments make it easier for children to understand scientific principles.

example, if playing with two identical balls of clay, they will no longer think that when one ball is rolled out into a sausage shape there is then more clay in it than in the other. Logical thought will prove to them that the amount of clay in each must still be the same, whatever the changes in appearance of the shapes in front of them.

These new developments in logic are accompanied by marked improvements in the organization of memory. When children of this age are faced with new problems, they may now be able to solve them using techniques or information learned when mastering previous, similar problems. If they are given important jobs to do, they are less likely to forget all about them if they then find something more interesting to get on with. Asked about something that may have happened some hours earlier, they can now get to the point much quicker without having first to work through everything else that occurred that day as well.

SCHOOL AND EDUCATION

These developments in logical thought mean that children can now be expected to think more about what they are learning and about why exactly they are learning it. So if they are studying wild life, children will no longer see animals in purely human terms. Instead they may start understanding the real pressures facing wild animals in their struggle for survival.

The ability to think about the past as well as the future now makes it possible for children to correct some of their own and their friends' mistakes through a process of step-by-step reasoning. Even so, most learning remains an active, practical affair, with children still benefiting most from experience with real objects in their lessons. Maths and early science are still best learned through observation and practical experiments. Children also learn a lot from each other by listening to different points of view, which is why many primary schools encourage children to work in groups. Even if they get the solution wrong, the process of discussion will still help them to understand that there may be more than one way of solving a problem.

MOTIVATION

What is it that makes one child more intelligent than another? There is no definite answer to this question, since experts still cannot work out to what extent children's intelligence is fixed at birth and how much this is influenced by their environment.

However, most experts in child development agree that while children may indeed be born with different capacities for intelligent thought, much will depend on how they are encouraged from then on to fulfil their potential. A few children seem to have a particular gift – for example in maths, music, art or chess – that cannot be explained by the way they have been brought up. But such skills may only become properly established if these children are encouraged to develop them.

Once a child is at school much depends on the type of teaching she experiences. If the atmosphere in the classroom is friendly and the lessons interesting, pupils will feel more like making an effort. A good teacher will quickly spot those areas in which each child needs special help and will then try to provide the right sort of stimulation. But if lessons are tense or badly organized, those children who need an extra push

A good teacher will recognize those areas in which a pupil needs extra help.

may either get overlooked or else feel so anxious that they spend their time wishing they could escape home or out into the playground.

THE *i*MPORT*a*NC*e* OF FR*i*ENDSH*i*P

While pre-school children spend relatively little time with others of their age, children between seven and eleven may spend up to half the day in the company of their age group. During weekends they may see twice as much of their friends as they do of their parents. Most friendships are formed between children of roughly the same age, height and range of interests. At a younger age, friendships can often change very quickly, but older children tend to stick more to the same friends.

Between the ages of seven and eleven, children may spend up to half their free time with friends.

Children who are depressed or neglected may find it difficult to make friends.

Some children find it hard to make friends, however much they would like to. Depressed children who may already be neglected at home will often have little to offer others by way of cheerfulness or entertainment. Emotionally disturbed children may also drive other children away with aggressive or attention-seeking behaviour. Such children find it increasingly difficult to make or keep any friends as they grow older. While children who make friends easily are able to practise and improve their conversational skills with their friends, develop their sensitivity to others and build up a general sense of trust, isolated children may never have the chance to get better in any of these areas.

SEX ROLES

In many societies men and women traditionally have different roles. For example, in many countries women are expected to look after the home and children. By ten years old, children have a strong sense of these roles. This may be reflected in their play; children of this age often play in single-sex groups.

MORALITY

Seven-year-old children tend to have very fixed ideas on what is right and wrong. For example, if they believe it is wrong to steal they will then think theft is always wrong, no matter what the circumstances. So they would think it wrong for a poor mother to steal some medicine she could not afford in order to keep her baby alive. However, at around ten years old children begin to understand that rigid moral rules can – and should be – broken in certain situations. They may also learn to take into account reasons why people behave in ways which may seem bad at first sight. Presented with one situation in which a child breaks

The increased strength that comes with late childhood brings a satisfying improvement in sporting skills for many youngsters.

one glass in a fit of temper, and another in which a child accidentally breaks ten glasses, seven-year-old children tend to believe that the child who broke ten glasses was the naughtiest. Older children faced with this situation will assess the intentions of both children, not just the results of their actions.

THE END OF CHILDHOOD

Between the ages of seven and eleven children grow five to seven centimetres each year on average. Weight also increases, and there is an improvement in the physical skills involved in sport. By the time they are eleven years old, some children will already be experiencing the first signs of adolescence, such as the rapid increase in growth that marks the transition into puberty. However, the experiences of childhood will remain with them, and may affect them for the rest of their lives.

SPECIAL NEEDS

WHILE THE majority of children develop in the way outlined in this book, there are a number of problems that can disrupt the normal course of development. This chapter looks briefly at some of the problems that might arise.

Some children may face developmental problems that mean they need special help in school.

CONGENITAL PROBLEMS

Congenital problems are those that are present at birth. They can arise through genetic problems, brain damage, or the failure of parts of the body to develop.

Down's syndrome is a congenital problem that affects about 1 child in 750. It occurs when a child is born with forty-seven chromosomes instead of the usual forty-six, and is more common in children of mothers over thirty-eight years of age. Children with Down's syndrome have certain characteristic facial features, such as widely separated eyes that slant upwards, and often have internal problems, particularly with their heart or bowels. Children with Down's syndrome do learn to stand, walk and talk, but this sometimes takes longer than usual.

autism

Autistic children find it difficult to communicate with other people, even though they may have average or above average intelligence. They may not recognize their parents or other familiar people, and may not communicate with speech, gestures or facial expressions. Some autistic children are silent and withdrawn, some mutter unintelligibly, and some are unpredictably violent. Children with autism have difficulty feeding and in being toilet trained. Some autistic children are particularly gifted in one area, such as music, art or maths.

No one is sure what causes autism. It may be present at birth or develop during the first few years

of life. It affects around 1 in 3,000 children, and is more common in boys. Some children recover from autism, but others need special care for their whole lives. Physical contact, such as holding and touching the child, and a lot of love and attention are thought to help.

Around one in four children do less well at school than they could.

accidents and infections

Accidents (in particular severe blows to the head) and some infections, such as polio and meningitis, can damage the brain and impair physical or mental development. In fact accidents are the main cause of death in children under five.

Learning difficulties

Apart from physical causes, such as illness, there are a number of reasons why children might have learning problems at school. Dyslexia is a term used to describe certain language problems, in particular slowness at learning to read and spell, characterized by reversing of letters in handwriting and difficulty in learning sequences such as days of the week. Although experts disagree about what dyslexia is and how it can be treated, children can overcome it if they are given special help.

Hyperactivity is a term that is often misused to describe children who are merely very lively and cannot sit still. True hyperactivity is rare, affecting only 1 child in every 1,000, and is sometimes the result of brain damage. Some experts believe that it can also be caused by allergies to certain foods and food additives.

Some children find difficulty in learning because of problems at home. While family crises such as divorce or death may affect a child's progress and concentration only temporarily, some children may be suffering severe and long-standing problems at home that will affect their school work. Children who

have been neglected when young may never have experienced the type of security that enables them to play happily by themselves. This can mean they have difficulties later on in concentrating at school. Instead of putting their energies into work, they may spend most of their time disturbing other children and annoying their teachers. Some children may retreat into day-dreams, sometimes becoming so quiet and withdrawn that pupils and teachers forget they are there at all.

Children who are physically or sexually abused at home are also likely to have problems at school. They may not trust any adult, even teachers who want to help them. These children often feel depressed, unwanted and worthless. Sometimes social workers or psychologists can help these children and their families.

At this centre, special techniques are used to help children overcome their developmental problems. Learning how to blow into this pipe may help this boy's speech problems.

These parents and teachers are discussing the best way to organize education in this school.

Around a quarter of all children do not do as well at school as they could. This may be due to problems already mentioned. On the other hand, it could also be because of lack of communication between their parents and teachers. Children with supportive parents, who encourage and take an interest in their children's school work, have the least problems at school. Children from homes where there is no interest in education may never feel encouraged to try. Bright, resourceful children may still succeed despite this, but others may not. Mindful of the special needs of these pupils, many schools now try to involve all parents in activities and discussion. Primary schools often invite parents into school, and teachers sometimes visit parents at home. In this way, ideas for educating and stimulating children can be shared.

CONCLUSION

Despite all our knowledge of child development, it is never possible to be absolutely sure about what makes one person different to another. It is also impossible to produce a perfect child to order. This is a very good thing. There are so many different and successful ways of bringing up children that no one has the right to tell parents exactly what they should do.

The best preparation for adolescence is a settled and contented childhood, during which a child has been encouraged to develop emotionally, intellectually and socially in an atmosphere that is warm and stimulating. However, no one can expect to have a perfect childhood or imagine that, because a few things have gone wrong, a child's future has been ruined. Many children manage to survive incredible hardships , and in fact facing problems and difficult situations is an important preparation for adult life.

The best preparation for adolescence is a contented childhood, during which a loving and stimulating environment has been provided.

GLOSS*a*RY

Adoption Bringing up someone else's child as your own and having this recognized legally.

Amniotic fluid The water in which a foetus floats inside the uterus before birth.

Chromosome A rod-shaped structure containing genes.

Conception The point when a male sperm fertilizes a female ovum.

Co-ordination Balanced and smooth movement.

Embryo A human being in the first two months of development in the uterus.

Foetus A human being from the end of the embryo stage of development to birth.

Fostering Looking after someone else's child as if she was your own for a limited period of time.

Gene A unit of heredity, passed on from parents to their children.

Immunity Protection from disease.

Inherit To have certain qualities passed on to you by parents, grandparents or other ancestors.

Labour The process of giving birth.

Ovum An egg produced in females, capable of growing into a baby if fertilized by a male sperm.

Placenta The organ through which a foetus feeds, breathes and gets rid of waste matter while in the uterus.

Sociable Friendly, enjoying the company of others.

Sperm A male cell, capable of fertilizing a female's ovum and producing a baby.

Stimulation Arousing the senses.

Tantrum A childish fit of rage.

Umbilical cord The cord that links a foetus with the placenta in the uterus.

Uterus The womb; the part of a woman's body in which a baby grows.

Values Those things that you think are important, such as honesty.

Zygote The cell formed when a female ovum is fertilized by a male sperm.

BOOKS AND VIDEOS

BOOKS

Garvey, Catherine *Children's Talk* (Fontana, 1984)
Garvey, Catherine *Play* (Fontana, 1986)
Minett, Pamela *Child Care and Development* (Murray, 1985)
Winnicott, D. W. *Babies and Their Mothers* (Free Association, 1988)
Woolfson, Richard *Understanding Your Child* (Faber, 1989)

VIDEOS

The following videos are available from Concord Video and Film Council, 201 Felixstowe Road, Ipswich, Suffolk, 1P3 9BJ:

Family Matters A series of films on the first two years of life.
Individual Differences: Infancy to Early Childhood The genetic and environmental influences that make each baby an individual.
The Psychology of the Pre-School Child Five children from around the world talk about their fears, interests, attitudes and dreams.
A Question of Sex – Child Rearing A mother and father reverse roles.
Sex Role Development Sex roles and stereotypes.

PICTURE ACKNOWLEDGEMENTS

ST. MARY'S R.C.
HIGH SCHOOL
RESOURCE BASE

The publisher would like to thank the following for provision of illustrations: J Allan Cash 4, 59; Cephas 34 (Nigel Blythe); Greg Evans 19, 38, 46, 50; Eye Ubiquitous 30, 31 (Yiorgos Nikiteas), 45 (Paul Seheult), 47 (Jex Cole), 54, 60 (Frank Leather); Format 8 (Raissa Page), 28 (Joanne O'Brien), 33 (Jenny Matthews), 40 (Joanne O'Brien), 48 (Mo Wilson), 52 (Raissa Page), 55 (Maggie Murray), 57 (Maggie Murray); Sally and Richard Greenhill 14, 26, 34; David Hoffman 61; Lesley Howling 25; John and Penny Hubley 22; Orde Eliason/Link 20, 37; Mozart Museum/Syndication International 5, 16; PHOTRI 5, 43; ZEFA 13. The artwork on pages 7 and 10 was provided by Peter Bull.

iNDeX